WITHDRAWN

HORSING AROUND

Rodeo

Robin Johnson

Crabtree Publishing Company

www.crabtreebooks.com

Crabtree Publishing Company

www.crabtreebooks.com

Author: Robin Johnson
Editor: Lynn Peppas
Proofreader: Crystal Sikkens
Editorial director: Kathy Middleton
Production coordinator: Katherine Berti
Prepress technician: Katherine Berti
Coordinating editor: Chester Fisher
Series editor: Sue Labella
Project manager: Kumar Kunal (Q2AMEDIA)
Art direction: Dibakar Acharjee (Q2AMEDIA)
Cover design: Tarang Saggar (Q2AMEDIA)
Design: Shruti Aggarwal (Q2AMEDIA)
Photo research: Ekta Sharma (Q2AMEDIA)
Reading consultant: Cecilia Minden, Ph.D.

Cover: A cowboy and his horse compete in a calf roping competition at Pikes Peak or Bust Rodeo in Colorado Springs, Colorado.

Title page: A competitor at the High School Boys and Girls Rodeo Competition, Port Huron, Michigan

Photographs:
Cover: James Frank/Jupiter Images (main image), Tischenko Irina/Shutterstock, Emberiza/Shutterstock, Shutterstock, P1: Dennis Macdonald/Photolibrary, P4: Nicholas Rjabow/Istockphoto, P5(b): Robert Harding/Masterfile, P5(t): Olivier Le Queinec/Shutterstock, Malibu Books/Shutterstock, James Nemec/Shutterstock, P6: North Wind Pictures/Photolibrary, P7(l): Olivier Le Queinec/Shutterstock, Malibu Books/Shutterstock, James Nemec/Shutterstock P7(r): Greg Kreller/Associated Press, P8: Alec Pytlowany/Masterfile, P9(l): Dennis Macdonald/Photolibrary, P9(r): Olivier Le Queinec/Shutterstock, Malibu Books/Shutterstock, James Nemec/Shutterstock, P10: Ron Hilton/Shutterstock, P11(t): Olivier Le Queinec/Shutterstock, Malibu Books/Shutterstock, James Nemec/Shutterstock, P11(b): Patrick Chatelain/Masterfile, P12: Toby Rankin/Masterfile, P13(t): Margo Harrison/Shutterstock, P13(b): Olivier Le Queinec/Shutterstock, Malibu Books/Shutterstock, James Nemec/Shutterstock, P14: Charles O Slavens/Photolibrary, P15(t): Olivier Le Queinec/Shutterstock, Malibu Books/Shutterstock, James Nemec/Shutterstock, P15(b): Lincoln Rogers/Shutterstock, P16: Kyle Carter/Reuters, P17: Olivier Le Queinec/Shutterstock, Malibu Books/Shutterstock, James Nemec/Shutterstock, P18: Photolibrary, P19(t): Craig Lister/Istockphoto, P19(b): Olivier Le Queinec/Shutterstock, Malibu Books/Shutterstock, James Nemec/Shutterstock, P20: Valpictures/Fotolia, P21(t): Paige White/Istockphoto, P21(b): Olivier Le Queinec/Shutterstock, Malibu Books/Shutterstock, James Nemec/Shutterstock, P22: Karl Weatherly/Photolibrary, P23(t): Ron Hilton/Shutterstock, P23(b): Olivier Le Queinec/Shutterstock, Malibu Books/Shutterstock, James Nemec/Shutterstock, P24: Rich Legg/Istockphoto, P25(t): Olivier Le Queinec/Shutterstock, Malibu Books/Shutterstock, James Nemec/Shutterstock, P25(b): Sergei Bachlakov/Shutterstock, P26: Jack Dempsey/Associated Press, P27(t): John Wood Photography/Getty Images, P27(b): Olivier Le Queinec/Shutterstock, Malibu Books/Shutterstock, James Nemec/Shutterstock, P28: Devere Helfrich Rodeo Photographic Collection, Dickinson Research Center, National Cowboy & Western Heritage Museum, Oklahoma City, Oklahoma, P29(l): Olivier Le Queinec/Shutterstock, Malibu Books/Shutterstock, James Nemec/Shutterstock, P29(r): Matt Sayles/Associated Press, P30: Douglas Peebles/Photolibrary, P31: Devere Helfrich Rodeo Photographic Collection, Dickinson Research Center, National Cowboy & Western Heritage Museum, Oklahoma City, Oklahoma, Folio Image: Wendy Kaveney Photography/Shutterstock

Illustrations:
Q2AMedia Art Bank : P17

Library and Archives Canada Cataloguing in Publication

Johnson, Robin (Robin R.)
    Rodeo / Robin Johnson.

(Horsing around)
Includes index.
ISBN 978-0-7787-4977-6 (bound).--ISBN 978-0-7787-4993-6 (pbk.)

    1. Rodeos--Juvenile literature. I. Title. II. Series: Horsing around (St. Catharines, Ont.)

GV1834.J64 2009   j791.8'4   C2009-903737-8

Library of Congress Cataloging-in-Publication Data

Johnson, Robin (Robin R.)
    Rodeo / Robin Johnson.
      p. cm. -- (Horsing around)
    Includes index.
    ISBN 978-0-7787-4993-6 (pbk. : alk. paper) -- ISBN 978-0-7787-4977-6 (reinforced library binding : alk. paper)
    1. Rodeos--Juvenile literature. I. Title. II. Series.

GV1834.J57 2010
791.8'4--dc22

                         2009023636

Crabtree Publishing Company

www.crabtreebooks.com   1-800-387-7650

Published in Canada
Crabtree Publishing
616 Welland Ave.
St. Catharines, ON
L2M 5V6

Published in the United States
Crabtree Publishing
PMB16A
350 Fifth Ave., Suite 3308
New York, NY 10118

Published in the United Kingdom
Crabtree Publishing
Maritime House
Basin Road North, Hove
BN41 1WR

Published in Australia
Crabtree Publishing
386 Mt. Alexander Rd.
Ascot Vale (Melbourne)
VIC 3032

Contents

Rodeo 101

Rodeos are rough-and-tumble shows! In rodeos, daring riders show off their skills. They compete against other riders, racers, and ropers in timed or roughstock events. Riders are often called cowboys or cowgirls.

In timed events, riders must complete a group of difficult moves quickly. The riders work with their horses to catch, tie, or wrestle calves, bulls, or other animals. Riders may also race quickly around a number of objects. Timed rodeo events include barrel racing or steer wrestling. Other events are tie-down roping and team roping.

In roughstock events, riders earn points by riding **broncs** or bulls. Broncs are horses that buck, or move their bodies up and down. They want to throw off the riders.

A bucking horse lowers its head, arches its back, throws its hindquarters up in the air, and kicks out its back legs.

Roughstock events include saddle bronc riding, bareback bronc riding, and bull riding. These events are fast and exciting. Rodeos are often big

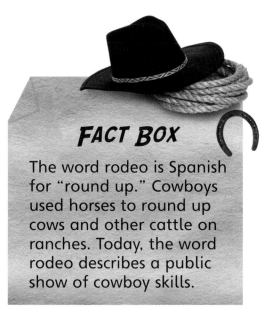

FACT BOX

The word rodeo is Spanish for "round up." Cowboys used horses to round up cows and other cattle on ranches. Today, the word rodeo describes a public show of cowboy skills.

Western-themed shows. Fans often come dressed in colorful cowboy clothes. They enjoy all sorts of entertainment. There might be music, parades, and carnivals. The chuckwagon races always draw a crowd. Riders move chuckwagons pulled by horses around barrels. Chuckwagons were used to pull cooking supplies in the Old West. The object of the race is to get the wagon around a number of barrels. Imagine driving a big horse-drawn wagon around a barrel!

Chuckwagon races are popular forms of entertainment at some rodeos.

History of Rodeo

In the Old West, ranchers had to herd, rope, tie, and care for their cattle. Cowboys challenged one another to complete their ranch duties quickly. Soon, cowboys were competing in shows.

In the early 1700s, Spanish settlers brought horses and cattle to North America. Spanish cowboys are called *vaqueros*. They set up ranches to raise the animals. The animals roamed freely across the land. North American cowboys began using horses to round up the wild cattle. In the 1820s, cowboys started competing against *vaqueros* in rodeo-type contests.

In 1872, the first official rodeo was held in Cheyenne, Wyoming. By the early 1900s, rodeos became popular forms of public entertainment. They were often combined with Western shows.

Big stars were Buffalo Bill Cody and sharpshooter Annie Oakley. Cheyenne Frontier Days, the Calgary Stampede, and the Pendleton Round-Up began to attract riders from around the world.

Cowboys and vaqueros displayed their riding and roping skills in early rodeo-type competitions.

The first indoor rodeo was held in Fort Worth, Texas in 1918. Women and men competed in early rodeos. The women wore heavy split skirts instead of pants. They took part in all events. In 1929, popular rider Bonnie McCarrol was killed in a fall. She was thrown from her horse in a roughstock event at the Pendleton Round-Up. After her death, women were no longer allowed in dangerous events at rodeos. Today, women compete only in barrel racing at major rodeos. They compete in both timed and roughstock events at rodeos only for women. Men compete in **wild rides** and showdown events.

This daring trick rider is showing her wild side and entertaining spectators at an early rodeo.

FACT BOX

Early rodeos were very different from rodeos today. Early rodeos included events such as trick and fancy riding. Trick riders performed gymnastic moves on galloping horses. In fancy riding, ropers first made fancy shapes with their ropes. The shapes helped them catch animals or people. Early roughstock events had no time limits. Some wild rides lasted for over ten minutes!

Rodeo Roundup

Early rodeos were held on ranches. Today, professional rodeos take place in large indoor or outdoor arenas. Arenas are enclosed areas surrounded by seating for viewers. Fans gather at rodeos to cheer for their favorite riders and horses.

The main part of a rodeo arena is the performance area. This is a big, flat, closed-in area that is covered with dirt. The performance area is usually rectangular in shape. A number of fenced boxes are attached to the arena. The boxes are called holding pens where competitors and animals wait before their events. Some boxes have gates that can be opened quickly.

The Calgary Stampede is the largest outdoor rodeo in the world. It is held every July in Alberta, Canada.

The National Finals Rodeo (NFR) is often called the World Series of Rodeo. It is an important event that takes place every year in Las Vegas, Nevada. Officials award World Championship titles. The All-Around title is given to the cowboy who has been the most successful in at least two events.

Rodeo is popular throughout much of the United States. This young rider is competing in a high school rodeo in Michigan.

Others have chutes that lead into the arena. Rodeos are held in arenas around the world. They are particularly popular in the western parts of the United States. Other locations are Canada, Mexico, and Australia. Some rodeos are small, local events. These are for **amateur** riders. Other rodeos are large events for professional athletes. Professional athletes are people who are paid to play their sports. These riders compete for big **purses** at international rodeos.

Time for Horses

There are horses in nearly every rodeo event. Horses must be fast, and work well with their riders. Here are a few of the timed events using horses.

In steer wrestling, a horseback rider chases a bull. He then jumps off his horse and wrestles the bull to the ground. Horses in this event are trained to keep running without their riders.

The horses must be able to run quickly for short distances. They can run from a standing start to about 150 feet (46 m) in four seconds!

Riders and horses race head over heels to win the team roping event.

Riders and horses work together in tie-down roping events. A rider chases and ropes a calf. The horse stops running so the rider can jump off. The rider quickly ties the calves' legs together. Meanwhile, the horse pulls back on the rope. This keeps the rope tight. Horses in this event must be quick, and smart.

Team roping is the only team event at rodeos. Two mounted riders work together to catch steers. The first is called the header. He ropes the front of the steer. Headers ride tall, heavy horses. This helps them hold and turn the large steers once they are caught. The second rider is called the heeler. He ropes the back of the steer. Heelers ride smaller horses. This helps them follow the steers and respond quickly to them.

FACT BOX

Steer wrestling is the most dangerous timed event. If a rider misses the steer, he could land on his head! The heavy steer could end up on top of the rider!

Saddle Bronc Riding

Saddle bronc riding is a true roughstock rodeo event. It began on ranches in the Old West. Cowboys tried to break wild horses. Breaking means taming horses so people can ride them.

The saddle bronc event takes courage. A rider tries to stay on a bucking horse for eight seconds. A rider may use only one hand to hold the braided reins. There are many ways a rider can get **disqualified** from the event:

1) he drops the reins,
2) his feet slip from the stirrups,
3) he is thrown from the horse,
4) he touches the horse, equipment, or himself with his free hand,
5) he doesn't mark out (see Fact Box).

The ride is over for this cowboy competing in the saddle bronc event.

12

This cowboy has saddled up for a wild ride on a bucking bronc.

In roughstock events, both riders and their horses earn points from judges. From two to four judges award the points. The points are added together. The highest score a horse and rider can receive is 100.

In saddle bronc competitions, horses score points for bucking wildly. Riders score points for disciplined rides. They also get points for the correct use of spurs. Their goal is to ride smoothly.

FACT BOX

A rider must begin the saddle bronc event with his heels touching the horse above its shoulders. The rider must keep his heels there until the front hoofs of the horse hit the ground out of the chute. This type of start is called marking out. It gives the horse the advantage in the event.

13

Bareback Bronc Riding

Bareback bronc riding is the wildest horse-riding event in rodeo. It is also the hardest on a rider's body. In this event, fearless riders try to ride bucking horses bareback. To ride bareback means to ride without a saddle.

In the bareback bronc event, a rider holds on to the handle of riggings with only one hand. Riggings are leather pads wrapped tightly around the horse's chest. A rider tries to stretch his feet forward during the ride. He then tries to roll his spurs back up toward the riggings. Riders earn points for spurring the horses high on their bodies. Riders are disqualified if they do not stay on the horses for eight seconds.

Bareback bronc riders hold tightly to riggings. They are the only things that keep riders from flying off the horses!

They are also disqualified if they touch anything with their free hand, or if they do not mark out. At least two other riders on well-trained horses are also in the arena. The riders stay close to the competitor. They help him if he is thrown from the bucking animal or if he needs help dismounting. Dismounting means to get off a horse.

FACT BOX

Bull riding is a daring roughstock event. It is often described as "the most dangerous eight seconds in sports." Bull riding is similar to the bareback bronc event. The difference is that a rider tries to ride a bull weighing more than a ton (1000 kg)! The rider can hold only the ropes tied around the bull.

Some competitors say that bareback bronc riding is like riding a jackhammer with one hand!

Barrel Racing

Barrel racing is the only women's event in professional rodeos. It is a timed race that requires **horsemanship** and speed. Cooperation between riders and their horses is also important.

A rider must move quickly through a barrel racing course. The course is made up of three large barrels at set distances apart. The barrels may be metal or plastic drums. A rider gallops across a score line to begin the race and start the clock. She must speed through the course and circle each of the three barrels one time. The rider may move through the course either to the left or right. She must circle the barrels in a cloverleaf pattern.

This horse and rider are speeding through a barrel racing event at a professional rodeo.

A rider who does not run the race in a complete cloverleaf pattern is disqualified. The race clock stops when the rider and horse cross the score line again.

The rider with the fastest time wins the barrel racing event. Only speed counts in this rodeo event. Points are not awarded for style or for skill. In professional rodeos, an electronic eye is at the score line. It records times to the hundredth of a second. An electronic eye is a timing device that shines a beam of light. The clock starts and stops when the beam is interrupted by the horse and rider. At smaller rodeo events, judges use timers to record race scores. Depending on the size of the courses, barrel racing times are usually between 12 and 18 seconds.

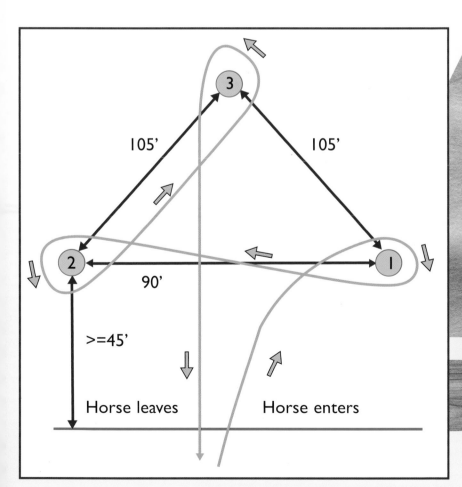

105'   105'

90'

>=45'

Horse leaves   Horse enters

FACT BOX

A rider may touch or move barrels during races. She can even grab barrels to prevent them from falling over. However, the rider must remain on her horse. Judges will add five-second penalties to total times if a rider knocks over any barrels during competition.

This diagram shows the cloverleaf pattern that must be followed in the barrel racing event.

Life in the Fast Lane

There are many types of horses used in different rodeo events. Horses used in timed events are fast and agile. They can complete difficult moves quickly and carefully. They need special care and training to stay fit and healthy.

American Quarter Horses are the most popular horses for timed events. They are strong, athletic horses with solid bodies. They can run very fast for short distances. Other breeds are Thoroughbreds, Appaloosas, and American Paint Horses. These are also good choices for timed rodeo events. Rodeo horses work hard. They must have extra protein in their diets. They need good-quality hay. Their feed should include oats and grass. They also need plenty of fresh water. They should be fed at least twice a day. Feedings should take place at least two to three hours before competitions.

American Quarter Horses are called the "World's Fastest Athletes." They have been clocked at speeds up to 55 mph (89 km/h)!

Most riders competing in timed events train with their horses during the week and travel with them to rodeos on weekends.

Riders should groom, or clean rodeo horses regularly. Riders should also wash and brush horses thoroughly before their events. They should use hoof picks to remove pebbles and dirt from the horses' hoofs. Pebbles could injure the horses or cause them to fall during speed events. Rodeo horses must be exercised at least five times a week. This keeps them fit and fast. Trotting up and down small hills helps build up horses' muscles and **stamina**. Horses training for speed events should practice their events in enclosed areas. They should also be given plenty of runs on trails.

FACT BOX

Horses travel to rodeos in trailers. Trailers should be clean and airy. There should be plenty of hay and water. Horses should wear leg wraps for protection. They need blankets for warmth when traveling. They should be allowed to leave the trailers every three to four hours. They need to get fresh air and stretch their legs.

Bucking Broncs

In the Old West, wild cats often attacked horses that roamed. The horses bucked to try to free themselves from their attackers. The instinct to buck off anything or anyone on their backs remains in horses today.

The word bronc comes from the Spanish word *bronco*, which means "rough." Rodeo broncs are rough, strong, spirited animals. They are not wild horses, however. Most rodeo broncs have been bred and trained to buck wildly. Some broncs are unbroken **domestic** horses. Trainers encourage the natural bucking instincts of horses. They reward them for throwing riders. Trainers also tame the horses so they can load them into trailers and take them to shows with other horses. For this reason, most rodeo broncs are **geldings**.

Broncs are assigned by chance to riders at rodeos. The competitor who gets this bucking horse is in for a wild ride!

This bronc is taking a break from rough-and-tumble rodeos. It is stopping to smell the flowers—and eat some tasty grass.

Geldings are gentler and easier to handle than **stallions**. Mares, or female horses, are also used in roughstock events.

American Quarter Horses, Appaloosas, and American Paint Horses are popular breeds of bucking horses. Broncs used in the bareback event are usually smaller horses with wild bucking styles. Broncs used in the saddle bronc event are large, sturdy horses. They are bigger than bareback broncs. They also have a more rhythmic bucking style.

Many saddle broncs are bred with draft horses. Draft horses are large, strong horses that can pull heavy loads.

FACT BOX

Most bucking broncs work in rodeos for only a few minutes a year! The rest of the time broncs usually live in herds on large ranches. Broncs' owners feed them well and groom them. Bucking horses are valuable animals. The best broncs are worth more than $50,000!

Ride Em' Cowboy!

Rodeo riders are tough, daring men and women. They must be strong, fast, and brave in the rodeo ring. They work hard and train for many years to become professionals in their sport.

Most professional rodeo competitors grow up on ranches. When they are young, they take care of horses and other cattle. They learn how to ride horses, throw ropes, and catch livestock. Many successful pro riders compete in rodeos on the weekends. Then they continue to work on ranches during the week.

You don't have to live on a ranch to become a rodeo rider. Cowboy schools and camps give people of all ages and skills chances to learn about horses from experts.

This young cowboy uses a dummy calf to practice roping skills.

This woman is training for a barrel race. She and her horse will soon be teaming up in a professional rodeo.

Beginners learn safe handling skills to use on ranches and in rodeos. More experienced students work to improve their skills for competitions.

Rodeo riders exercise to stay fit and strong. They compete in amateur rodeos to gain skill. Then it's off to professional rodeos where they must perform like champs!

FACT BOX

Cowboys do all sorts of things to prepare for rodeos! Roughstock superstar Ty Murray practiced gymnastics. He walked on fences for miles and learned how to juggle. He even learned how to ride a unicycle to improve his balance!

23

Horse Tack and Cowboy Hats

Horses require special tack, or equipment, to take part in rodeos. Riders also wear special gear to compete in rodeo events. These pages explain the coverings of rodeo horses and riders.

Rodeo competitors use Western-style tack. They sit on a leather saddle, or seat that is strapped to the back of the horse. The rider puts his or her feet in stirrups that are attached to the saddle. The rider holds on to straps called reins. The reins are attached to a bridle. A bridle is a group of straps that fit over the horse's head. Bridles allow riders to guide and control their horses. Rodeo riders wear long-sleeved shirts. They wear jeans or other sturdy long pants.

hat

chaps

saddle

boots

Cowboy clothes are tough and sturdy. They are made to handle the wear and tear of rodeo life.

Leather leggings called chaps go over the riders' pants to help protect their legs. They wear cowboy boots on their feet. Big, wide-brimmed cowboy hats sit on their heads. Women wear the same type of clothing as men. Women's clothes often have more color. They may also have tassels, sequins, or other decorations.

Most rodeo riders wear spurs on their boots. Spurs are small, pointed objects that encourage horses to move. In some events, riders may carry lariats. Lariats are stiff ropes with loops. Riders throw lariats around animals and pull to tighten the ropes.

Western tack allows riders to stay on their horses as they race through challenging rodeo events.

FACT BOX

For timed events, riders use standard Western saddles with high backs and horns in front. In the saddle bronc event, riders use special saddles that do not have horns. The horns are removed from the saddles so riders do not injure themselves.

Risky Business

Rodeo is a dangerous sport. Each year rodeo riders, horses, and other livestock are injured or killed in events. Some people believe that rodeos are cruel and should be banned, or not allowed. Others feel that competitors should be allowed to practice their sport.

People who **protest** rodeos say that animals are being harmed for human entertainment. They say that broncs and bulls especially are treated cruelly in roughstock competitions.

Riders in those events use flank straps. These are wide leather straps tied around the animals' bodies in front of their back legs. Flank straps encourage animals to buck. Protestors claim that competitors pull flank straps tightly around the animals. They say this causes animals pain and injury.

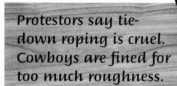

Protestors say tie-down roping is cruel. Cowboys are fined for too much roughness.

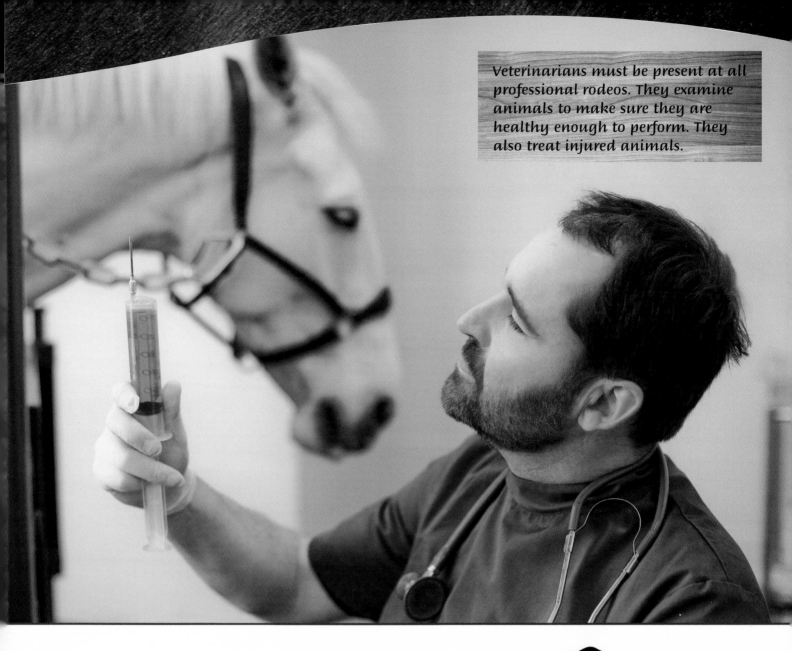

Veterinarians must be present at all professional rodeos. They examine animals to make sure they are healthy enough to perform. They also treat injured animals.

Defenders of rodeo say that only strong, healthy animals will perform well in the rodeo arena. They argue that broncs and bulls will not buck if they are afraid or in pain. In fact, the animals will refuse to move or will try to run away from the pain. They say that flank straps are harmless belts lined with sheepskin or other soft materials. They say that rodeos use flank straps to encourage bucking animals to kick their back legs straighter and higher.

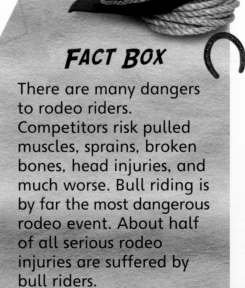

FACT BOX

There are many dangers to rodeo riders. Competitors risk pulled muscles, sprains, broken bones, head injuries, and much worse. Bull riding is by far the most dangerous rodeo event. About half of all serious rodeo injuries are suffered by bull riders.

27

The Best of the West

To be successful in rodeos, competitors must be strong, fast, and fearless. Their riders must be pretty good, too! Read on about some of the most famous horses and cowboys of the rodeo world.

Midnight was a saddle bronc superstar of the 1920s and 1930s. The black gelding was a Morgan and Percheron cross. He was famous for throwing off all but a handful of riders. It is believed that only five riders were able to complete a saddle bronc event on Midnight! This horse and his owner, rodeo great Verne Elliott, have been inducted into the ProRodeo Hall of Fame.

Baby Doll Combs was a champion Quarter Horse. She competed in steer wrestling events in the 1950s. Her riders earned over $400,000 in prize money.

Baby Doll Combs was a short brown mare. She was well suited for steer wrestling and won many prizes in the event.

Baby Doll's owner, Willard Combs, allowed other steer wrestlers to ride her. He would get part of their winnings. In 1957, Baby Doll carried Combs to first place as the World Champion Steer Wrestler. She carried other riders in that event who placed second, third, fourth, and fifth!

Ty Murray is known in the rodeo world as the "King of the Cowboys." Murray began breaking wild horses when he was eight years old. He ruled saddle bronc, bareback bronc, and bull-riding events for many years. In 1998, he became the first cowboy to win the All-Around title seven times!

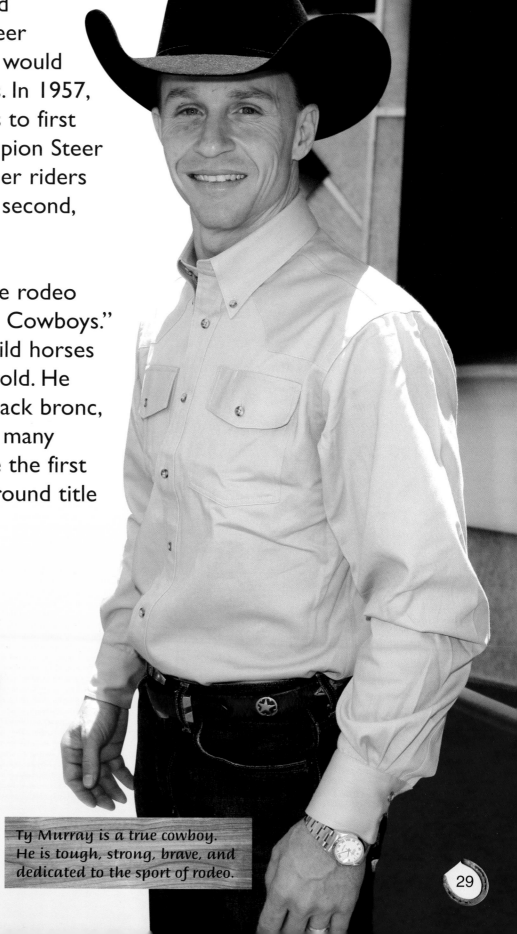

FACT BOX

The ProRodeo Hall of Fame honors important contributions to the sport of rodeo. It opened in Colorado in 1979. Since then 206 people, 25 animals, and 16 rodeos have been inducted, or admitted as members.

Ty Murray is a true cowboy. He is tough, strong, brave, and dedicated to the sport of rodeo.

Facts and Figures

Rodeos test the speed, skill, and strength of both riders and horses. Read on for some cool competitive world records!

Top Marks

1. The highest score ever given in a roughstock event was a perfect 100 in bull riding. It was earned by Wade Leslie riding Growney's Wolfman in 1991.

2. The highest score ever given in the saddle bronc event was 95 points. Two riders and their horses earned that score. It happened once in 1979 and another time in 1996.

3. The highest score ever earned in the bareback bronc event was 94 out of 100. It was achieved by two different competitors in 2002 and 2003.

Over 600 professional rodeos are held in the United States each year.

Speed Limits

1. Steer wrestling is the fastest rodeo event. Typical professional times for the event are 3.5 to 10 seconds. The current world record is only 2.4 seconds!

2. The fastest time for the team roping event is 3.5 seconds.

3. The fastest time for the tie-down roping event is 5.7 seconds.

Money Talks

1. Over $12 million in prize money is awarded at rodeos each year.

2. The largest purse ever won at a single rodeo was $142,644. It was won by B. J. Schumacher at the 2006 Wrangler National Finals Rodeo.

3. The most money ever won in a single year of competition was $425,115. It was won by Trevor Brazile in 2007.

Champion Spirit

1. The youngest World Champion was Jim Rodriguez Jr. He captured the team roper title at just 18 years of age.

2. The oldest World Champion was Ike Rude. He roped the World Champion title at the age of 59.

3. The record for the most World Rodeo titles goes to Jim Shoulders. He had a total of 16!

Jim Shoulders was head and shoulders above the competition.

Glossary

amateur Describing someone who plays a sport for fun

bronc Short for bronco; an unbroken or slightly broken range horse

disqualified To be eliminated from competition for not following the rules

domestic Describing an animal that is trained to live with people

gelding A male horse that can no longer breed to produce a foal

horsemanship The skill of riding and handling horses

protest To publicly say or show that you are against something

purses Prize money won at rodeo events

stallion An adult male horse that can breed to produce a foal

stamina The strength and energy to do something for long periods of time

wild ride A fast ride on a bucking horse or bull

Index

Printed in the U.S.A.—CG